Gail Rubin

WITH A CAMERA

Photographs of a Biblical Safari

ABBEVILLE PRESS · PUBLISHERS · NEW YORK

Designed by Andor Braun

All biblical citations from *The Holy Scriptures According to Masoretic Text* (Volumes I and II).
Copyright © 1955 by the Jewish Publication Society of America, Philadelphia, Pennsylvania.

Photograph on page two © by "Ben-Tsion" Allan Cisco

Library of Congress Catalog Card Number: 79-5086
ISBN 0-89659-076-3 (cloth)
ISBN 0-89659-071-2 (paper)

FOURTH PRINTING

for Mary
a mixture of Israel and photography
wishing you a happy time here
and all the best
Anna.
27. August 1986.

Gail Rubin

PSALMIST
WITH
A CAMERA

GAIL RUBIN

PSALMIST

Text by GAIL RUBIN

Introduction and additional text by Rabbi MICHAEL GRAETZ

Foreword by General (Reserve) AVRAHAM YOFFE

Contents

Introduction

GAIL RUBIN was a psalmist with a camera. She wanted to reveal the mystery and the sublimity inherent in every creature. It was no accident that she fell in love with Israel, land of the Bible. She saw its rocks, trees, flowers, and animals through the eyes of a seer of mystery. She felt the inner harmony and the overwhelming beauty of each creature. She strived to reveal that life and earth are woven together in a pattern that is discernable through sensitivity as well as science. In revealing this pattern to us, she lifts our spirits to joy, and this joy brings praise to our lips. These are the insights of the psalmist, which enabled him, through his vision of nature, to sing the praises of the Almighty.

These insights made Gail turn her camera into an instrument whereby this vision of the beauty and harmony of nature could reveal the joy of life. In her photographs one senses her rapture at seeing the texture of tree bark, the blend of purple and green in anemone and grass, or the majesty of a bird in flight. To show us this, she needed inordinate patience. She would remain for hours, eyes fixed on a tree, waiting for a young stork to make its first flight. She had a sense of being present at the day of creation. Development of life was her deepest inspiration. Her animals are less often seen alone than in families or groups — she discerned within nature a love pervading all the universe, a love which for her was expressed even in rock formations and trees. For Gail Rubin beauty and love were the same.

She searched the Bible for references to animals and plants and found in it the relationship between animals, land, and history. She was proud that modern Israel had restored the wildlife of the Bible. For centuries Palestine was poor in plant and animal life, but Jewish settlement reversed this process, and cultivation of the land brought back the migratory birds of biblical times. In Beer Toviah Gail found a pair of nesting storks who came back year after year. She called them the "annual tourists."

Gail regretted that most people bypassed nature preserves in favor of elegant buildings or historical sights, not realizing that biblical Israel's animal and plant life could be seen once again. She hoped that her photographs would lead people to sense deeply the land of the Bible by walking through its fields.

Her work succeeds. It has the magical quality of inspiring the viewer, so that he will walk in the fields and see the world as he had never seen it before. One who has seen her photographs can never again read the prophets or the psalms without visualizing the harmony and beauty they reveal. In that sense she joins in the long history and tradition of biblical exegetes whose insights illumine the Scriptures. With the psalmist she says, "I will sing praise to my God while I have any being."

RABBI MICHAEL GRAETZ

Foreword

WHEN the band of terrorists landed on the shore near Ma'agan Michael, the first thing they saw was a young woman photographing birds in flight, birds nesting, and nestlings being fed their evening meal by their mothers. After questioning her as to the name of the place where they had landed, they murdered her in cold blood.

She was a young woman from the United States who had settled in Israel in 1969. I had seen her first in 1975, in the New York office of the Holy Land Conservation Fund, and it was then that I made the acquaintance of Gail Rubin. During our talk she told me about her dream, her wish to photograph the landscape, animals, birds, and everything else connected with nature in Israel. My first impression was that I was talking with a person who knew exactly what she wanted to do. I saw samples of her work, and they impressed me profoundly. There and then I invited her to come to the Nature Reserves Authority, pledging to give her every possible help to start her off on her new project in Israel.

A few months later, Gail appeared in my office, and with her modest bearing, her innate shyness and reluctance to draw attention to herself, asked me how she could be of help to the Nature Reserves Authority. I explained that we were lacking a person with photographic talents such as hers, one who could capture with a camera the beauty of Israel's landscapes, trees, birds, animals, and other natural assets. We then talked at length about what places she should visit and where she should tour to collect first impressions. I advised her to concentrate on two places, for a start: first, the Hai-Bar Biblical Wildlife Reserve in the Arava, situated 50 kms north of Eilat—a reserve intended for the restoration of species of animals already extinct in Israel, remnants of which, however, are still extant in various corners of the earth, and specimens of which we are bringing to Hai-Bar for breeding; and second, the Hula Nature Reserve in the north, which is a stopover place for tens of thousands of birds on their long migratory flights in autumn from Northern Europe and Asia to the hot countries in Africa, and back along the same route in the spring. I explained to Gail that pictures such as hers would help us endear these birds and animals to the Israeli public, youth and grown-ups alike, and induce them to take part in the great task of nature preservation in which we in the land of the Bible are engaged. Gail's face lit up with a shy smile; she thanked me and, equipped with introductions to the various reserve wardens, set out on her way. This second meeting with Gail strengthened in me the conviction that we had a forthright, candid person of outstanding qualities.

I didn't see Gail for several months, and when she came to see me again she approached me with a certain hesitance, as though wanting to apologize for troubling me. She had no idea how glad I was to see her. After talking together about her experiences, her tours, and the sights she had seen, she opened her big portfolio and drew out whole sets of slides she had taken during the previous months. I remember how stunned I was by the quality of her slides, by the play of light and shade, the clearness and sharpness of detail, and her grasp of the distinctive characteristics of the country with its too bright light and its too dark shade. If during our first meeting I had been struck by her shyness and reticence, this time I could discern in her signs of enthusiasm which had not been apparent before; and I felt that she had gained greater self-confidence and had become more certain of what she wanted to achieve and how she was going to go about it. At once I saw the raw material that would help us bring to the public our ideas about nature conservation, and draw attention—at home as well as overseas—to the beauty of Israel's nature and natural assets.

Thus, quietly and unobtrusively, Gail became one of us, enriching our life with her wonderful photographs. One day, I saw her sitting and waiting for me outside my office,

and when I asked her why she had not come in, she smiled and told me that she hadn't wanted to disturb me. After I had invited her in, she showed me some new pictures, and then, with eyes gleaming hilariously, drew out a number of slides, put them before me and asked, "What do you think of this?" After a while, when I had failed to identify the subject, she told me with a smile that they were pictures of the bark of the eucalyptus tree. These slides—some of which were later published in an American magazine—are a good example of what an artist can make of a nature subject, which other people will heedlessly pass by. In the course of time, Gail gave the Nature Reserves Authority a good many pictures and slides for purposes of information and education.

The last time I saw Gail was when she came to my house at my invitation one evening when I was showing a nature film on Namibia. She had brought along her big portfolio with samples of enlargements of her pictures. Again I noticed how she was shrinking from the crowd. Her modest bearing, and the light in her eyes on that evening will remain with me always.

I shall remember Gail as one who came to us to enrich us, and whose span of life was cut short in so tragic a way, leaving us bereaved, with nature and nature preservation in Israel deprived of her invaluable photographic contributions.

AVRAHAM YOFFE, General (Reserve)
Chairman, Israel Nature Reserves Authority

Gail Rubin

PSALMIST
WITH
A CAMERA

Mount Hermon

BEHOLD, HE SHALL SWOOP AS A VULTURE
AND SHALL SPREAD OUT HIS WINGS.
(Jeremiah 48:40)

Griffon Vulture

The griffon vulture soars above the gorges and ravines of the Golan Heights, where, high in the hills, this predator builds its nests. Its majestic wingspan — as long as ten feet — is captured in this photograph, taken from below, near Mount Hermon.

THE ROCKS ARE A REFUGE FOR THE
CONIES. *(Psalms 104:18)*

Conies

The cony, also known as the hyrax, is a small African mammal
weighing five to seven pounds when mature. Conies frequent rocky,
scrub-covered areas, the most northern of which is on the
Israeli-Syrian border. The cony is a distant relative of the elephant,
evidenced by its tusklike upper incisors and arrangement of limb
bones. However, the two animals share no common ancestor later
than the Eocene epoch, forty-five million years ago.

The great nature Psalm 104 sings of the harmony and purpose
within creation, emphasizing that the Creator has provided each
creature with its particular sustenance and its particular home. The
psalmist finds as one of the prime examples of God's harmony the
small cony, whose home is the large, craggy rocks of the hill
country.

... FROM THE MOUNTAINS OF
THE LEOPARDS.   *(Song of Songs 4:8)*

Mount Hermon

The highest mountain in the Golan Heights, Mount Hermon is at present Israel's northernmost border. Leopards still prowl the mountain, as they did in biblical times.

Patches of snow linger well into the summer near the peak's basalt-rock summit. In this photograph snow contrasts with the dark basalt rocks to form a striking abstraction of black and white.

As the snows melt, they filter through the rocks, and in the absence of real soil on the mountain, the melting snow appears as springs at the bottom of the mountain, feeding the Jordan River and making the piedmont a green, well-watered area.

FOR, LO, THE WINTER IS PAST, THE RAIN IS
OVER AND GONE, THE FLOWERS APPEAR
ON THE EARTH.   *(Song of Songs 2:11–12)*

Anemones

After the first rains in December and January, the fields are alive
with the vivid colors of wild flowers. Among the first to bloom is
the delicate anemone. This flower, known in modern Hebrew as the
Kolanit, is considered the "national folk flower" of Israel.

Hula Nature Reserve

PELICAN

WATER BUFFALO

MONARCH BUTTERFLY

HULA WATERSCAPE

TURTLEDOVE

ALBINO SPARROW

... LIKE A PELICAN OF THE WILDERNESS;
I AM BECOME AS AN OWL OF THE WASTE
PLACES.   *(Psalms 102:7)*

Pelican

From early October until mid–November thousands of migrating
pelicans stop in the Hula swamps to rest and fish, much as they have
done since biblical times. Waves of pelicans darken the sky each
afternoon as they swoop down on clumps of papyrus.

... A GREAT FEAST, UPON THE MOUNTAINS
OF ISRAEL ... THE FLESH OF THE MIGHTY
SHALL YE EAT ... RAMS, LAMBS, AND
GOATS, BULLOCKS, FATLINGS OF BASHAN ...
(Ezekiel 39:17–18)

Water Buffalo

This powerful animal was used for both work and food in biblical
times, and if it is the biblical *meri*, as some scholars think, then it is
the animal used for sacrifices by the people of Israel in the time of
King David.

. . . AND THAT WHICH THE CANKER-WORM
HATH LEFT HATH THE CATERPILLAR EATEN.
(Joel 1:4)

Monarch Butterfly

The striking orange of the monarch butterfly is seen here against the
grass and flowers whose pollen provides nourishment. An
accomplished flier and glider, the monarch is a famous long-distance
migrant. Despite the large and lovely flocks of butterflies that
migrate to Israel regularly, the Bible is strangely silent about this
insect.

DARKNESS OF WATERS, THICK CLOUDS OF
THE SKIES.   *(Psalms* 18:12*)*

Hula Waterscape

Gail loved the Hula Lake area for its very wildness, which was just out of the setting of ancient Israel and had been spared modernization. She spent much time there in the piece of wilderness left as a reminder of what once was in the area.

Her words on the Hula
speak better than anything else:

The Hula Nature Reserve is the 700-acre remains of the original Hula Valley swamps and lake. Located in the basinlike depression ten miles north of the Galilee city of Tiberias, it is surrounded by Golan Plateau on the east and Naftali Ridge on the west. One of the foremost dreams of the Zionist pioneers was to drain the Hula swamps, kill off the notorious malarial mosquito (Anopheles), and reclaim the alluvial soil for farm use by neighboring settlements. Swamp drainage started in the early 1950s. But what was a farmer's dream became an ecologist's nightmare. The balance of life was upset. The natural order destroyed. The interrelationship of amphibian, mammal, and birdlife and swamp vegatation vanished. As reed, papyrus, lotus, and water lily disappeared, so did life dependent on it—snail, fish, water turtle, mongoose, jungle cat, wild boar, and water buffalo. But the most spectacular and disturbing change was the abrupt decline of migratory birds resting in the secluded swamps during their long European-African flight and back. The vast swamplands, once the scene of constantly changing birdlife—ducks, herons, pelicans—fell silent.

A group of nature-loving kibbutzniks waged a heroic struggle to save part of the Hula as an example of an ancient past. They lobbied in the Israeli parliament, wrote letters to newspapers, argued with whomever would listen to them, and finally in desperation banged on Ben Gurion's door and pleaded with the Israeli leader. A reprieve to total drainage was granted. And, in 1957, the southern part of the former swamps was granted official status as a nature reserve. Strict laws of animal and bird protection were soon instituted.

... THE FLOWERS APPEAR ON THE EARTH;
THE TIME OF SINGING IS COME, AND THE
VOICE OF THE TURTLE IS HEARD IN OUR
LAND ...   *(Song of Songs 2:12)*

Turtledove

The turtledove is a migrant bird, and it is the messenger of spring,
the season of its arrival in Israel.
The meek and gentle turtledove appears in the Psalms as a metaphor
for innocent Israel, beset by its predatory enemies.

YEA, THE SPARROW HATH FOUND A HOUSE
... WHERE SHE MAY LAY HER YOUNG ..."

(Psalms 84:4)

Albino Sparrow

The sparrow is one of the most common birds in Israel and is found
in all seasons of the year. It nests in stones of buildings and in the
eaves of rooftops; it is also found nesting in the stones of the
Western Wall. The albino sparrow is an uncommon variety.

Sinai Desert

LIKE CRAWLING THINGS OF THE EARTH
THEY SHALL COME TREMBLING OUT OF
THEIR CLOSE PLACES . . .   *(Micah 7:17)*

Sinai Agama

The blue agama—a slender, delicate lizard—is native to the southern Sinai desert. The male turns electric blue, as seen in this photograph, during the June mating season.

. . . WHEN THOU HAS BROUGHT FORTH THE
PEOPLE OUT OF EGYPT, YE SHALL SERVE
GOD UPON THIS MOUNTAIN.

(Exodus 3:12)

Sinai Mountains

In the Bible there are many names for Mount Sinai — "The
Mountain of God," "The Mountain of Horeb," among them — and
it is not clear if all the references are to the same spot, nor has the
exact location of Mount Sinai been discovered. The Jebel Musa,
known as Mount Sinai today, and at whose foot lies St. Catherine's
Monastery, was identified as Mount Sinai by Christian monks as
early as the second century A.D.
After a long and strenous climb up the granite slopes of the Sinai
range, one is rewarded with this awesome view.

... SOW NOT AMONG THORNS ...
(Jeremiah 4:3)

Echinops Thistle

The hardy echinops thistle grows between the rocks of Mount
Moses. Thistles and thorns were as common to the Israeli landscape
in biblical times as they are today. These are stately plants with fine
petite flowers, but after a period of time they dry up and become
hard, brittle, and sharp.

Gail was fascinated with these beautiful flowering thistles, which can
become dangerous hazards. She often walked in the fields of the
nature reserve at Ramat ha-Nadiv near Zichron Yaakov, looking at
the thistles and thorns, which grow so abundantly in that
well-watered area.

THE BURDEN OF THE WILDERNESS OF THE SEA.
(Isaiah 21)

Sharm el-Sheikh

Sharm el-Sheikh is not mentioned in the Bible, but the area was well traveled by people in biblical times. It is a strategic promontory, overlooking the Strait of Tiran near the southern tip of Sinai, at the mouth of the Gulf of Aquaba.
The photograph captures the blend of subtle colors of the sea and the land.

THE DAUGHTER OF MY PEOPLE IS BECOME
CRUEL, LIKE THE OSTRICHES IN THE
WILDERNESS.   *(Lamentations 4:3)*

Ostrich Rock Drawing

The existence of ostriches in the desert area in ancient times in attested to by the rock drawings found in the Sinai desert. These drawings also suggest that the desert area was once fertile.

Eucalyptus Treebark

LET THE FIELD EXULT, AND ALL THAT IS
THEREIN: THEN SHALL ALL THE TREES OF
THE WOOD SING FOR JOY . . .

(Psalms 96:12)

Eucalyptus Treebark

The Australian blue-gum eucalyptus tree was first brought to Israel
over eighty years ago by the French philanthropist Baron Edmond
de Rothschild to help Zionist pioneers drain the swamps. A
fast-growing tree that reaches maturity in five years, it was later used
to forest barren hills and to serve as a windbreaker screen around
Negev desert crops.

Gail's discovery of the aesthetic possibilities of eucalyptus treebark
was one of the great epiphanies of her life. She would visit this
grove frequently to see how the colors of the bark were developing.
Many times she would go without her camera, "just to see how the
colors were blending."

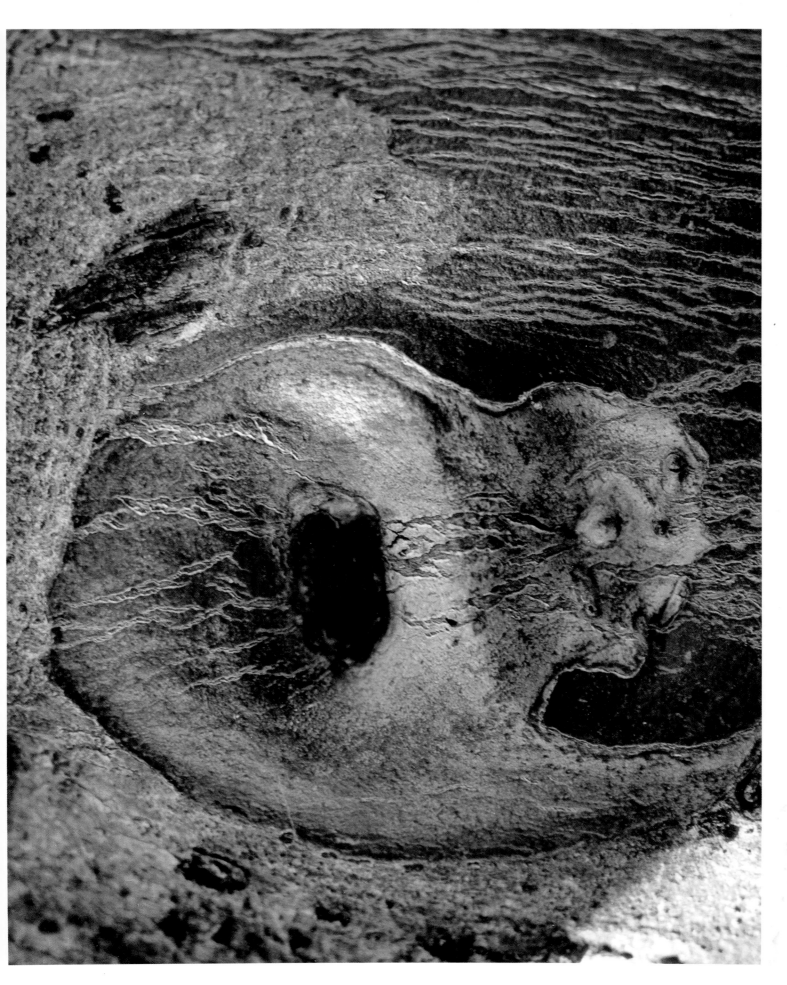

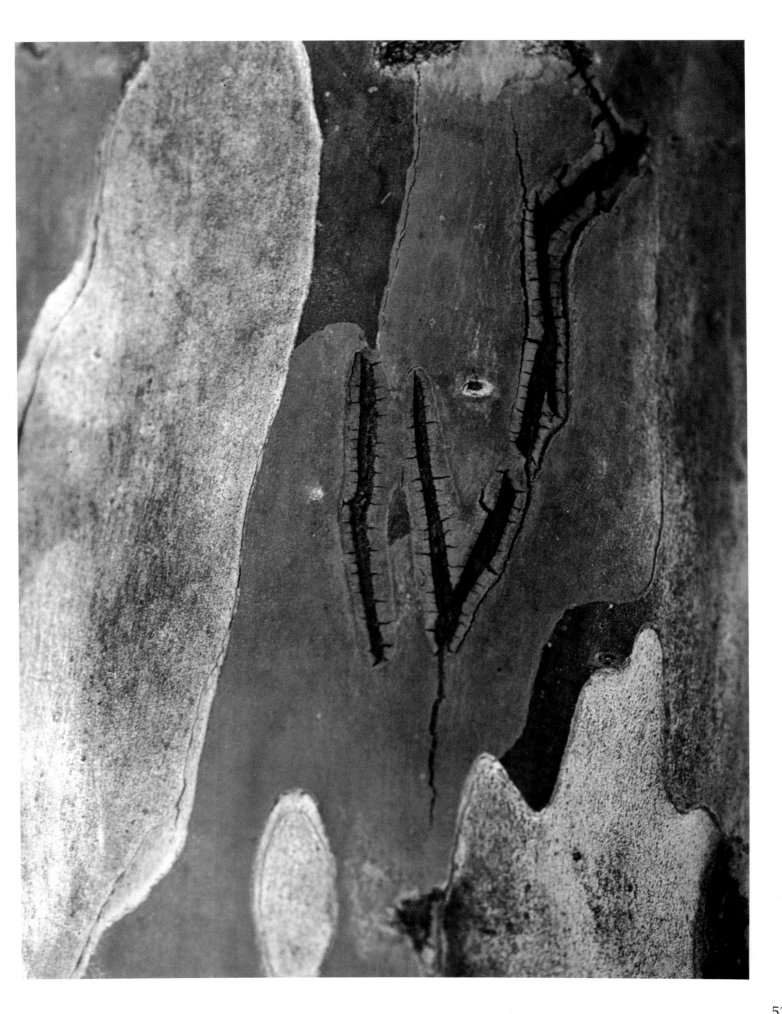

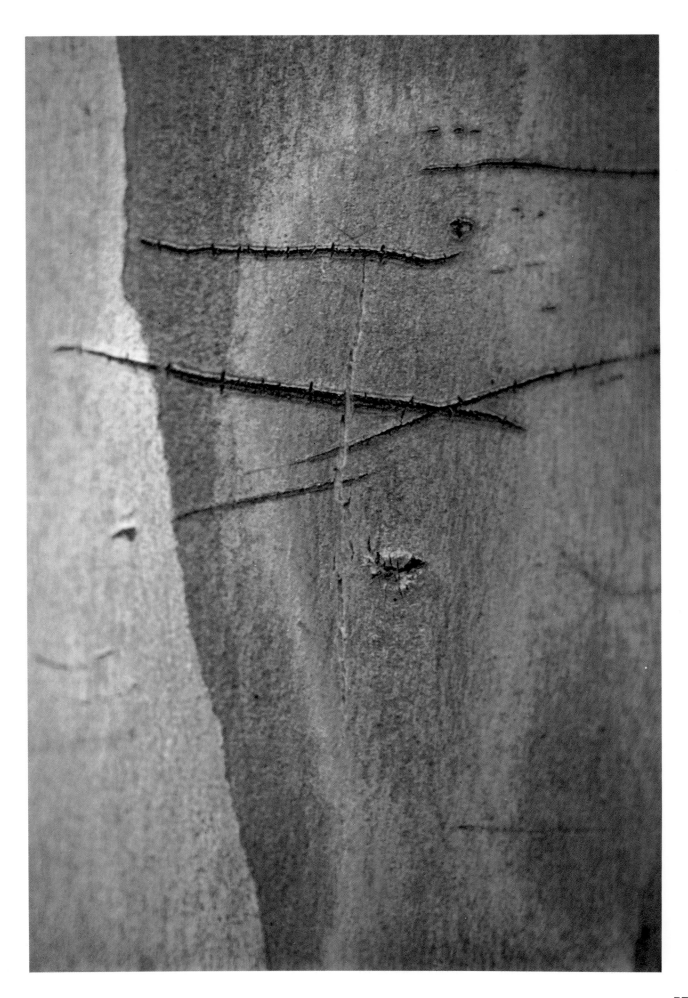

Hai-Bar Nature Reserve–Arava Valley

ADDAX

SCIMITAR-HORNED SAHARA ORYX

PERSIAN ONAGERS

SOMALI WILD ASS

OSTRICHES

FOX

THESE ARE THE BEASTS WHICH YE MAY EAT
... THE PYGARG ...

(Deuteronomy 14: 4–5)

Addax

The addax, which is identified as the pygarg in the Septuagint translation of the Scriptures, is native to the North African deserts. Its short, thick legs and broad hooves are particularly adapted to traveling on sand. They survive by their remarkable ability to scent grass newly sprouted by the infrequent desert rains.

The addax normally travels in pairs or small herds, and this "family portrait" was a special favorite of Gail's.

... MY HORN HAST THOU EXALTED LIKE
THE HORN OF THE WILD OX ...

(Psalms 92:11)

Scimitar-horned Sahara Oryx

The scimitar-horned Sahara oryx is probably the antelope that gave rise to the unicorn myth, for when viewed in profile it appears to have only one horn.

It is a species well adapted to desert survival. It can go for long periods without water, and like the addax, it feeds on desert grasses and scrub.

The oryx was hunted in biblical times for its hide and flesh. Up until recent times nets were used to capture this extremely dangerous and sharp-horned animal. In the twentieth century, however, automobiles have been used for hunting the oryx, and as a consequence, it has been hunted almost to extinction.

A WILD ASS USED TO THE WILDERNESS,
THAT SNUFFETH UP THE WIND IN HER
DESIRE . . ."   *(Jeremiah 2:24)*

Persian Onagers

The Persian onager, a seriously endangered species, has replaced the extinct Syrian onager on which, according to legend, Jesus rode into Jerusalem on Palm Sunday. For many centuries it was hunted for sport by the Persian nobility, and young onagers were captured for the breeding of riding animals.

REJOICE GREATLY, O DAUGHTER OF ZION,
SHOUT, O DAUGHTER OF JERUSALEM;
BEHOLD THY KING COMETH UNTO THEE,
HE IS TRIUMPHANT, AND VICTORIOUS,
LOWLY, AND RIDING UPON AN ASS,
EVEN UPON A COLT THE FOAL OF AN ASS.

(Zechariah 9:9)

Somali Wild Ass

This species of ass is probably related to the *bamor* or *aton* in biblical Hebrew. In the Bible the ass is spoken of as a means of transportation.

THE WING OF THE OSTRICH BEATETH
JOYOUSLY . . .   *(Job* 39:13-18)

Ostriches

The ostrich is one of the few flightless birds. The Syrian species, which lived in biblical times and became extinct at the turn of the twentieth century, was considerably shorter than the seven-foot-tall African ostrich.

FOR THE MOUNTAIN OF ZION, WHICH IS
DESOLATE, THE FOXES WALK UPON IT."

(Lamentations 5:18)

 Fox

The fox still lives in Israel as it did in biblical times. There are
several types of foxes, including the diminutive fennec fox pictured
here.

Its biblical portrayals are far different from the gentle mood of this
photograph. In the Bible, the fox is pictured as the inhabitant of
ruins, and its presence is a sign of desolation. They are also pictured
as scavengers, prowling the wastelands for food.

Ein Gedi Oasis

COMMON BULBUL

NUBIAN IBEX

SALT FORMATIONS

LOT'S WIFE

DEAD SEA

NEGEV DESERT

SHEEP

FOR, LO, THE WINTER IS PAST . . .
THE TIME OF SINGING IS COME . . .

(Song of Songs 2:12)

Common Bulbul

The Bible's lyrical description of winter's passing and the arrival of spring speaks of the period when the songbirds are heard. The Hebrew word apparently refers to songbirds of many types, including the common bulbul. These birds become preoccupied with nesting during the spring, and at mating time the whole land is filled with their song.

THE HIGH MOUNTAINS ARE FOR THE WILD
GOATS . . .   *(Psalms* 104:18)

Nubian Ibex

The Sudanese oasis zone at Ein Gedi, on the shores of the Dead Sea, is a tropical enclave in the barren wastes of the Judean desert. The steep limestone cliffs of the wadis are home to herds of ibex, a nimble-footed goat that makes startling vertical leaps up the sheer cliff walls.

A SALT LAND AND NOT INHABITED . . .
(Jeremiah 17:6)

Salt Formations

The Dead Sea is usually referred to in the Bible as the "Salt Sea." The formations pictured here are the product of the salts of the sea water. Because of the area's hot climate and low altitude — it is the lowest spot in the world — the sea water evaporates quickly leaving the salts exposed in large, glittering fields.

... SHE BECAME A PILLAR OF SALT.

(Genesis 19:26)

Lot's Wife

The story of Lot's wife is connected with the salt formations around the Dead Sea since this was probably the area in which lay the Cities of the Plains destroyed by God's wrath. There are many stories about the salt formations, and one persistent tradition is that this particular formation is itself Lot's wife, turned to salt as she looked back at the destruction of Sodom and Gommorah.

IN WHOSE HANDS ARE THE DEPTHS OF THE
EARTH: THE HEIGHTS OF THE MOUNTAINS
ARE HIS ALSO. THE SEA IS HIS AND HE
MADE IT: AND HIS HANDS FORMED THE DRY
LAND.   *(Psalms 95: 4–5)*

Dead Sea

The Dead Sea is situated between steep and rocky cliffs, rising up to
4000 feet. The sea is fed chiefly by the Jordan River, and there is no
outlet. Today, the inflow has been greatly reduced by the increased
use of the waters of the Jordon for irrigation. One of the saltiest seas
in the world, the Dead Sea supports no life, but it does yield salts,
"farmed" by present-day inhabitants of the area.

... IN THE WILDERNESS SHALL WATERS
BREAK OUT, AND STREAMS IN THE DESERT.

(Isaiah 35:6)

Negev Desert

The southern area of Israel from Beer Sheba south is known, as it was in biblical times, as the Negev. Negev means "dry, unwatered land," and this aptly describes the Negev during most of the year. After the winter rains, however, the usually dry river beds run with water, and the brown Negev is turned, momentarily, into a green and fertile land.

WE ARE THE PEOPLE OF HIS PASTURE, AND
THE FLOCK OF HIS HAND.

(Psalms 95:7)

Sheep

Sheep are among the most numerous animals in all regions of Israel,
and in modern Israel the Bedouin are the main herders of sheep. As
in ancient times, the sheep are raised for meat and for their wool.
This flock of sheep and their shepherd were photographed in the
Negev, where Gail spent time among the Bedouin.

Hill Region near the Jordan Valley

SHORT-TOED EAGLE

GAZELLES

FLOWERING ALMOND TREE

CHRYSANTHEMUMS

HYSSOP

... THEY SHALL MOUNT UP WITH WINGS AS
EAGLES ...   *(Isaiah 40:31)*

Short-toed Eagle

This soaring, winged predator abounds in Israel. Its white, speckled
body contrasts strikingly with the deep blue of the sky.
The short-toed eagle feeds mainly on snakes, and for that reason its
numbers remain abundant. Other eagles eat rodents, which in turn
eat chemically treated crops, and these eagles have recently decreased
dramatically in number.

HARK! MY BELOVED! BEHOLD, HE COMETH,
LEAPING UPON THE MOUNTAINS, SKIPPING
UPON THE HILLS. MY BELOVED IS LIKE A
GAZELLE OR A YOUNG HART.

(Song of Songs 2:8–9)

Gazelles

South of the Sea of Galilee is the hot plateau of the Jordan Valley.
For thousands of years the hills of Yisacher, banking the valley, have
been inhabited only by herds of gazelles, whose hooves made them
impervious to the bite of the deadly Palestinian viper, which is
plentiful in the region.

Gail's photograph is the result of setting up a "hide" at Ramat
Yisacher and waiting patiently, cramped in the small "hide," for the
gazelles to come and drink from the spring. Here, she has
photographed a couple, traveling together after the courting season.

... AND THE ALMOND TREE SHALL
BLOSSOM ...   (*Ecclesiastes* 12:5)

Flowering Almond Tree

These photographs of the almond tree were taken during the tree's first flowering—right after the winter rains. The almond is the earliest of all trees to flower in Israel, and it signals the beginning of the "New Year of the Trees," the fifteenth of the Hebrew month of Shevat.

ALL FLESH IS GRASS, AND ALL THE
GOODLINESS THEREOF IS AS THE FLOWER
OF THE FIELD; THE GRASS WITHERETH, THE
FLOWER FADETH . . .   *(Isaiah 40:6–7)*

Chrysanthemums

Gail's photograph captures the ephemeral yellow of the wild
chrysanthenums, which blossom between mid-January and late
March in the hills of Samaria.
As in most of her pictures of flowers, the background is as important
to the picture as the flower itself. The green of the wild grass in
Israel is the background of many of her photographs of wild flowers.

... AND HE SPOKE OF TREES, FROM THE
CEDAR THAT IS IN LEBANON EVEN UNTO
THE HYSSOP THAT SPRINGETH OUT OF THE
WALL ...   *(I Kings 5:13)*

Hyssop

The hyssop is a shrub that grows between rocks and stone walls,
which are found throughout Israel. This shrub, although hardly
exotic, was used as an element in many of the most important rites
of purification found in the Bible.

Mediterranean Coastal Fishponds

STORKS

EGRETS

CHAMELEON

MUSTARD FLOWERS

SEA GULL

GULLS

SPOONBILLS

... THE STORK IN THE HEAVEN KNOWETH
HER APPOINTED TIMES ...

(Jeremiah 8:7)

Storks

The twenty-year-old fishponds of the kibbutz and moshav collective settlements along the Mediterranean coast support a wide range of water birds. According to the annual water-fowl count made each January 15 by the rangers of the Nature Reserve Authority (a government agency) and the Nature Protection Society (a citizens group) there has been a steep rise in the number of fowls wintering in Israel; they had formerly migrated to Africa. This rise has resulted from the establishment of the fishponds, the institution of laws for wildlife protection, and the increase in amount of irrigated land and water areas.

Of this particular photograph Gail noted, "The white stork couple have nested in the same tree for the last four years. Each year the male comes to inspect the nest in late February, making whatever repairs are necessary and adding to the nest. Two weeks later he leaves to collect his mate, and shortly thereafter they both return for the eggs to be laid."

BEASTS, AND ALL CATTLE, CREEPING
THINGS AND WINGED FOWL ... LET THEM
PRAISE THE NAME OF THE LORD ...
(Psalms 148:10–13)

Egrets

The egrets are water birds that live around the fish ponds or in marshes. The white, or "snowy," egret was for a time hunted almost to extinction for its white plumage. This darker egret, never widely hunted, has managed to survive in large numbers. They thrive now in the ponds of the Mediterranean coast in Israel, where they winter, migrating back to Europe to nest in spring.

AND THESE ARE THE THINGS WHICH ARE
UNCLEAN UNTO YOU AMONG THE
SWARMING THINGS . . . THE CHAMELEON.

(Leviticus 11:29–30)

Chameleon

Gail's photograph depicts the chameleon well disguised by green
leaves. Its habit of changing skin color to blend into the immediate
surroundings is well known. One can watch a chameleon in Israel
leave his leafy perch and go onto the ground or even the road, and
change in the process from green to black.

IN DAYS TO COME SHALL JACOB TAKE
ROOT, ISRAEL SHALL BLOSSOM AND BUD;
AND THE FACE OF THE WORLD SHALL BE
FILLED WITH FRUITAGE.   *(Isaiah 27:6)*

Mustard Flowers

The mustard flowers are typical of the wild flowers in the winter.
These tall and graceful yellow flowers are found in great abundance
throughout Israel, reminding one of the prophecy of Isaiah.
Although not mentioned in the Bible, the mustard plant, which
grows wild virtually throughout modern Israel, was apparently
cultivated in Mishnaic times—from the third century B.C. to the
third century A.D.

FOR A BIRD OF THE AIR SHALL CARRY THE
VOICE . . . *(Ecclesiastes* 10:20)

Sea Gull

The sea gull eats fish and scavenges for food, usually around bodies
of water. In Israel, however, it is also known to go inland, even to
the Negev, where it eats land snails.
The gull's graceful line in flight is revealed in Gail's photograph.

LET FOWL FLY ABOVE THE EARTH IN THE
OPEN FIRMAMENT OF HEAVEN.

(Genesis 1:20)

Gulls

The long, narrow wings of the gull and its webbed feet enable it both to soar and to swim. Here, a flock of gulls is returning to the beaches along the Mediterranean coast.

BEASTS, AND ALL CATTLE, CREEPING
THINGS AND WINGED FOWL ... LET THEM
PRAISE THE NAME OF THE LORD ...
(Psalms 148:10, 11)

Spoonbills

The attraction of an ever greater number of waterfowl to
Israel—drawn by the fishponds established along the coast—was a
source of joy and satisfaction to Gail. Her favorite way of relaxing
was to drive to one of the kibbutz fishponds and photograph the
graceful movements of the waterfowl.

ABOUT GAIL RUBIN

GAIL RUBIN was born in New York City on April 12th, 1938. She graduated from the Dalton School in 1956, went to the University of Michigan, and graduated from Finch College in New York in 1960. She then entered the publishing field where she worked in an editorial capacity for Viking Press and New Directions before becoming managing editor of Delacorte Books.

In June of 1969 she went to Israel for a three-week vacation and was so taken by the country that she decided to stay on for a year. Her stay lengthened into almost nine years, when she was shot down by terrorists on March 11, 1978.

Her interest in photography led to professional work in 1972, when she became a photojournalist working mainly in black-and-white, with occasional work in color. After the 1973 war, she decided that the hectic pace of photojournalism did not suit her temperament, and she began to concentrate on nature photography in color. Her color photographs have appeared in NATURAL HISTORY, U.S. CAMERA, TIME-LIFE *Nature Science Annual 1976*, TIME-LIFE *Birds of Sea, Shore and Stream, Life in Zoos and Preserves,* and TIME-LIFE *Photography Annual 1979.*

Her work has been exhibited at the Israel Museum in Jerusalem and at the Jewish Museum in New York. The latter exhibition is currently touring the United States, as are the photographs which have been shown at the Magnes Museum in Berkeley, California.